LITTLE MONSTER'S ALPHABET BOOK

by Mercer Mayer

to Anne

MERRIGOLD PRESS • NEW YORK

© 1978 Mercer Mayer. Little Monster is a trademark of Mercer Mayer.
All rights reserved. Printed in the U.S.A.
No part of this book may be reproduced or copied in any form without
written permission from the publisher. All other trademarks are the property of Merrigold Press.
Library of Congress Catalog Card Number: 77-90978 ISBN: 0-307-03938-2 MCMXCI

I have an
alphabet collection.
There is something in it for
every letter of the alphabet.

Aa

is a brown, grumpy
apple that's been
on the ground
all winter.

Bb
is a balloon I collected
from Dr. Windbag on my last visit.

Cc

is for color. I collect something for every color in the rainbow.
You can remember all the colors of the rainbow by making a name out of them:

RED **O**RANGE **Y**ELLOW **G**REEN **B**LUE **I**NDIGO **V**IOLET

YELLOW
hat

ORANGE
orange

VIOLET
grapes

RED
wagon

BLUE
overalls

INDIGO
an Indigo Snake

GREEN
unripe bananas

Dd is a dragon and they are much too big to collect so I collected a duck instead.

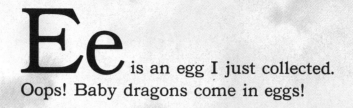

Ee
is an egg I just collected.
Oops! Baby dragons come in eggs!

Ff is a field of fireflies. I collect some in a jar, but I let them go before I go inside.

Gg is for the games I like to play.

Hh is for helping.
How many ways can you help?

Ii is for insect. I have a pet ladybug and a cricket, but I don't want a pet spider.

Jj is a jester. I have a jester costume and I tell jokes. I also collect jelly beans and I eat them as fast as I can collect them.

Kk is a key. I collect keys.

Ll is the lock on my secret chest, but I have so many keys that I never can find the right one.

Mm is my magnet.
I collect things that stick to my magnet.

Nn is a nut. Squirrels collect nuts to store in their nests for the winter.

Oo

is for anything old. I have lots of old stuff in my collection. Right now I have my old overalls on because I'm painting a picture.

Pp

old can

old chair

old shoe

old overalls

Sometimes I use a brush and sometimes I use my fingers. It's much more fun to use my fingers.

Qq is a question. I collect questions to ask my Grandpa.

Rr is my red rubber raft.

Ss is the sea,

a ship on the sea,
a snail and some shells on the beach.
I have five shells in the S-part of my alphabet collection.

Tt

Tt is my collection of toys—my toy-trunk, top, train, truck, and tricycle.

Uu

Uu is something useless. I can't think of anything to use it for, but it's real neat.

Vv

Vv is a visit from Grandma and Grandpa on Valentine's Day.
I collect visits on other days, too, like my birthday and Christmas.

Ww is collecting wheels in my wagon.

Xx is the skull and crossbones flag flying from my pirate ship.

Yy is my yellow yo-yo.

Zz

is my Zipperump-a-zoo. I take him to see all the other strange creatures in Professor Wormbog's Monster Zoo.

Why don't you start
your own alphabet collection?